Together

creating family traditions

Together

creating family traditions

rondi hillstrom davis
janell sewall oakes

NINE
TWENTY
PRESS

acknowledgements

Photographers: Chet Morrison, Thomas Alcala, Henry S. Kranzler, Danielle Johnston, Ron Nance, Pat Haverfield-Haverfield Studios, and Masano Kawana-Photonica.

A special thanks to: Scott McFadden, Nicole, Witt, Haden, Bergen, Lauren, Dante, Elena, Lisa, Hannah, Kailyn, Aurora, Claudia, Max, Sue, Andrew, Maggie, Audrey, Alice, Pat, Annie, Taylor, Sarah, Megan, Taylor, Mitzi, Kit, Cole, Katie, Ben, Lucy, Hailey, Dana, Rex, Reed, Laura, Hannah, Grace, Will, Gabrielle, Emily, Scott, Brian, Hunter, Greg, Jeff, Sarah, Travis, Zack, Jenny, T.J., Joshua, Chandler, Raven, Joseph, and to Joe and John for their patience and technical support.

Together creating family traditions

P.O. Box 7748, Dallas, TX 75209-0748
1.800.825.6448 www.togetherparenting.com

International Standard Book Number
0-9716002-0-1

Library of Congress Control Number
2001119991

Distributed to the book trade in the
United States by Midpoint Trade Books, Inc.
1.212.727.0190

Book Design: Terrace Publishing

Printed in China by Asia Pacific Offset, Inc.

Published in the United States by NineTwentyPress
Foreign Rights Available

First Edition   10 9 8 7 6 5 4 3 2 1

dedication

For Jenny, Alice, Witt, and Haden.

I look through your eyes and I am a child again.

table of contents

Word of encouragement

On crisp autumn days, amber light filters through the trees creating long shadows. Children with rosy cheeks play among the scattered leaves and collect nuts like squirrels preparing for a long winter. The children return home with small treasures to share with their family. As time passes, the afternoon's walk becomes the catalyst for a multitude of activities. Together, parent and child will gild the cache of nuts, string them into holiday garlands, and present them as gifts to family and friends. In later years, their most enduring memories will be of these small moments they shared together.

The world of nature is full of adventure and discovery. An afternoon of play turns into a treasure hunt. Small details become important. When we slow down to see the world through a child's eye, we turn our attention away from the commercial marketing of holidays to a more personal expression of the season.

By relating our experiences, we hope to inspire you to create your own journal of personal traditions and holiday memories. Many of the projects in *Together* extend beyond one day. They are a culmination of a series of events that take you through nature, exploring and learning about plants, animals and what happens to the world as the seasons change. As your family seeks out the objects needed for an activity, you will inevitably notice the changes in nature that each holiday seems to bring.

The activities in *Together* go beyond what is typically expected of children. A child can just as easily string a garland of gilded walnuts as he can string a necklace of stale macaroni. In this book, simple techniques, distinct, natural materials, and a child's inventiveness yield surprisingly beautiful keepsakes.

Recipes are an important part of each chapter. Passed down from one generation to the next, recipes are one of the most cherished traditions. They often conjure up memories of holiday preparations or time spent with a favorite grandmother. Cooking provides a quiet time to pass on the wisdom of family lore.

The purpose of this book is to enrich the quality of time that you spend with your family. Each chapter has a journal page that encourages you to reflect upon and share your own family's traditions. Here, your family can journal together. Personalize the book. Make it your own. Use it to hold a special note, a snapshot, or a pressed flower. Write in the margins. Record cherished recipes. This year, shape the memories that will become milestones to look back upon. We hope this will inspire you to share the gift of time together.

Before you start

Take our ideas as inspiration. Make them your own by using what's around you. Improvise. There is no one way to do these projects. They are intended to provide unique opportunities for you and your child to explore the world together.

We designed these projects to be shared by both parent and child. Create a safe environment for your child. Make sure that you are on hand to supervise as they learn to work with a variety of tools and new techniques.

Think through the process before you begin. Read the directions and organize all the supplies first.

Create a winning situation for your child. Don't give her more to do than she can successfully handle. Let your child be the guide. Gauge the length of each session to her ability and attention span. You can set part of a project aside for another day.

Remember that your goal is to spend time together. Don't emphasize the product so much that you forget to enjoy the process.

Whimsical colors dance like snowflakes through the air.

the New year

Every year, on New Year's Day, four generations of the Sewall family gather at my parent's home in the country. Cousins, great-grandparents, brothers, and sisters make the annual trek to welcome in the New Year.

Throughout the day, my grandfather watches over a large pot of his signature gumbo, our New Year's tradition for luck and prosperity. The rich smell of Cajun spices permeates the air. As a child, I stood on a little red stool and helped him stir. When asked his recipe, Papa Frank simply answered, "It's all in the roux."

As we stirred, he told me the story of a stranger he met as a boy, while fishing in the backwoods of Louisiana. Year after year, this old Cajun and my grandfather returned to the same fishing hole. In a big, black, cast-iron skillet, Papa learned the secrets of making authentic seafood gumbo.

The tradition of relating family stories is still important to our New Year's Day celebrations. My father delights in telling the tale of the day that he and his brother trapped a squirrel and turned it loose in the house during my grandmother's bridge party. The ladies screamed as the boys chased the animal through the parlor.

Each year, the retelling becomes more embellished, and it never fails to get a rise out of my grandmother. I think she enjoys the laughter that their teasing initiates. In our home, the New Year begins with the sound of laughter.

A year of wishes.

new beginnings

*Cast your
wishes to
the wind.*

Most of us would define goals as objectives that are within our control to attain. Wishes, on the other hand, are our hopes and our dreams. It might seem impractical, but we still throw pennies into fountains and long for our wishes to come true. The activities in this chapter offer a different take on standard New Year's resolutions. They introduce your family to goal setting in a fun, child-friendly way.

Begin at dinner by discussing your own wishes and asking other family members to do the same. Give everyone a day or two to organize their thoughts, then gather in the room where your family feels most comfortable and begin to write. Let each person write as much (or as little) as they want. Leave a piece of paper on the breakfast table or in the car in case someone is suddenly inspired. Remember that dreams are very personal. Encourage everyone to share ideas without adding the slightest criticism or suggestion. When you give children the freedom to express themselves, they are more likely to confide in you.

By writing and sharing your dreams and aspirations you make them real. Let your enthusiasm motivate you. Often, the greatest reward is not the destination but the journey itself.

wishing tree

The start of each calendar year is a wonderful time to celebrate life and new beginnings. It is no wonder so many of us choose this time to set goals for ourselves. The wishing tree visually proclaims your hopes for the future. Have family members inscribe thoughts on colorful ribbons. Tie the ribbons to a barren winter tree. Listen to them whisper their messages as they flutter in the wind.

before you start

Gather together 8 ½ x 11-inch colored card stock, a hole punch, string, scissors, your family, and their wishes.

directions

1. Let each person choose a different color of bright card stock. You will need several sheets of each color.

2. Cut strips 2-inches wide by 8½-inches long. Using a hole punch, make a hole at the top of each strip.

3. Cut a 10-inch length of string for each colored tag. To make a loop, thread one end of the string through the hole and tie a knot.

4. Have each family member write their wishes on the tags.

5. Hang the wishes over the branches of a designated tree and announce your dreams to the world.

Dante and Max race through the snow.

New beginnings, new traditions.

pinwheels

before you start

Gather together colored paper, a penny, scissors, a ball head straight pin, a glass bead, a pencil with an eraser, your personal goals, and a spirit of adventure.

directions

1. Start with a 4-inch square of brightly colored paper. Use a sturdy paper if you plan to put the pinwheels outdoors. Write your goals on both sides of the paper.

2. Label the corners of your square A, B, C, and D. Draw a diagonal line from corner A to C, and from corner B to D. Place a penny in the center where the lines cross. Trace around the penny.

3. Cut along the lines from the corners to the center circle. Be sure not to cut through the circle. Each corner now has two points. Fold, but don't crease, the first point in corner A over the center circle. Alternate points around the square. Fold the first B over A, the first C over B, and the first D over C.

4. Push a long straight pin with a ball head through the center of the square. Slip a $\frac{1}{4}$-inch bead onto the pin behind the pinwheel. Stick the pin into the eraser of a pencil.

Place your pinwheels in a bank of snow and declare your goals to the world.

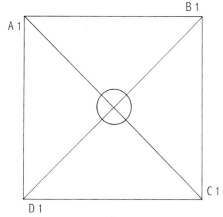

Enliven the winter landscape with these playful wheels of color.

chocolate truffles

ingredients

1 (12-ounce) package semi-sweet chocolate chips

$1/2$ cup heavy cream

1 stick ($1/2$ cup) unsalted butter, softened

4 tablespoons hazelnut syrup (available at gourmet coffee shops and specialty stores)

Unsweetened, powdered cocoa

directions

1. In a heavy saucepan, bring the cream to a boil, stirring constantly. Reduce it by half.

2. Remove from the heat. Add the chocolate and the hazelnut syrup. Stir over low heat until the chocolate has melted.

3. Whisk in the softened butter until the mixture is smooth.

4. Pour into a shallow pan and refrigerate 1 hour until firm.

5. Use a melon baller to scoop and shape the chocolate into 1-inch balls. Roll in unsweetened cocoa.

chocolate resolutions

Greet your guests with good wishes for the coming year. These small packages make great favors for a New Year's Day party.

before you start

Gather together 24 or more walnuts, hammer, awl, $9\frac{1}{2}$-yards of $\frac{1}{8}$-inch velvet ribbon, 1 sheet of $8\frac{1}{2}$ x 11-inch paper, and a permanent marker.

directions

1. With an adult, use an awl and a small hammer to gently pry the walnut shells open. Scoop out the insides and reserve the two shells. Keep each pair of shells together. Some may break. Have plenty of walnuts on hand.

2. Cut the paper into strips, $\frac{1}{4}$-inch wide and 2-inches long.

3. Using a permanent marker, write your New Year's resolutions or greetings on the slips of paper. Make sure the ink is dry.

4. Place a chocolate truffle inside each walnut half. Tuck a message inside. Cover with the other half of the walnut.

5. Cut the ribbon into 12-inch lengths. Lay the walnut on top of a 12-inch length of ribbon. Temporarily secure the ribbon to the bottom of the shell with a piece of tape. Carefully tie a bow around the walnut and remove the tape. Refrigerate until ready for use.

Place a bowl of these diminutive gifts near the front door or at the end of a buffet line for a surprise treat.

good luck gumbo

ingredients

1 pound uncooked mild andoule or Italian sausage

1 pound skinless chicken breast, bone in

4 cups chicken broth

4 cups water

3 bay leaves

1 teaspoon thyme

$\frac{1}{2}$ cup vegetable oil

1 cup flour

$1\frac{1}{2}$ cups onion, diced

$1\frac{1}{2}$ cups celery, diced

4 cloves garlic, minced

2 (14-ounce) cans stewed tomatoes

$1\frac{1}{2}$ teaspoons salt

1 teaspoon bottled hot pepper sauce

1 tablespoon gumbo filé

directions

1. In a large stockpot, combine the sausage, chicken, broth, water, bay leaves, and thyme. Bring to a boil. Reduce heat to low and simmer for 20 minutes. Cover, remove from heat, and leave 2 hours to cool and to let the flavors blend.

2. Chop the onion, celery, and the garlic. (Small, serrated paring knives are easiest for children to handle.)

3. The secret to making rich, flavorful soup is the roux. Combine oil and flour in a large skillet. Cook over medium heat, stirring constantly, until it is the color of cocoa powder (about 25 minutes). I usually put a spoonful of cocoa next to my skillet to compare the color. It is also very important to keep the roux from burning. Enlist a partner and stir in shifts.

4. Add onion, celery, and garlic. Stir for 5-7 minutes, or until the onions are almost transparent. Remove from the heat.

5. Remove the chicken, sausage, and bay leaves from the broth. De-bone and chop the chicken. Slice the sausage. Discard the bay leaves. Reheat the broth over medium heat.

6. Stir the roux into the warm broth. Add the chicken, sausage, tomatoes, salt, and hot pepper sauce. Continue cooking over medium heat for 5 minutes. Add the filé and cook 5 minutes more. Serve over rice.

My New Year's Day ritual always involved sharing the duty of stirring the roux with my grandfather.

This year, shout your dreams from the mountaintops.

reflect

Recipes are a great way to pass
on family traditions. Can you recall
a favorite recipe?

Does your family have any foods
that symbolize good luck?

How did you learn to cook?

What makes your family
gatherings memorable?

together

Encourage each member of your
family to make notes in this book.

These are some things I hope we'll
do together....

Maggie beams with pride as she presents a Valentine to her favorite teacher.

Valentine's day

One of my fondest childhood memories is of my mother helping me make a Valentine's box to take to school. We pulled out white paste, an old shoebox, scraps of doilies, and construction paper. There was a flurry of activity as I cut and pasted, and imagined my box filled with homemade Valentines from classmates and secret admirers.

My favorite teacher in the fourth grade was Mrs. Dearing. It was my job to clean the erasers after school. This was our excuse to talk. For Valentine's Day, I wanted to make her something special. My mother had a recipe for sugar cookies that she had made as a child. We stayed up late rolling out the dough, long after my brothers had gone to bed. Carefully, we sprinkled the cookies with sugar and waited for the sparkling wafers to emerge from the oven.

To this day, when I smell sugar cookies baking, I think about Valentine's Day and that special present for my teacher.

Golden brown and sparkling, this sugar cookie box is as delectable as it is charming.

sugar cookie box

ingredients

$1/2$ cup unsalted butter at room temperature

$1/2$ cup sugar

1 egg

$1/8$ teaspoon salt

1 teaspoon vanilla

2 cups flour

$1/2$ cup powdered sugar

$1^1/2$ teaspoons water

Granulated sugar for decoration

1 heart shaped cake pan (6 or 9-inches wide)

1 ceramic cookie mold (available where you find baking supplies)

directions

1. In a medium sized mixing bowl, cream together the butter and the sugar. Stir in the egg and vanilla. Mix in the flour and salt. Work it into a dough.

2. To make the box, coat the inside of a small, heart shaped cake pan with cooking spray. Press the cookie dough into the bottom and the sides of the pan until you have a layer $1/8$-inch thick. Chill the pan for 30 minutes. Reserve remaining dough for the lid.

3. Make the lid by rolling out the remaining dough between two sheets of wax paper. Roll to $1/8$-inch thickness. With a table knife, cut a heart out of the dough that is slightly larger than your heart pan. You can use the bottom of the pan as a guide. Peel the heart off of the wax paper and transfer to a greased baking sheet. Sprinkle with sugar and chill for 30 minutes. Reserve remaining dough.

4. Using a ceramic cookie mold, make a fancy cookie to decorate the lid. Coat the mold with cooking spray. Pour a little granulated sugar into the mold, tilt until sugar covers the bottom, and tap out any excess. Press dough into the mold and turn it out onto a greased baking sheet. Sprinkle with sugar and chill for 30 minutes.

5. Preheat the oven to 350°. Bake all chilled cookie pieces for 18-20 minutes, until golden. Cool completely.

6. Mix the powdered sugar and water in a small bowl. Use this mixture to glue the pressed cookie to the box lid. Fill the box with pastille candies and decorate it with sugared violets or a ribbon.

Instead of store bought Valentines, encourage your child to make a gift that will fill him with pride and accomplishment.

One taste of this candy immediately brings back memories of Grandma's kitchen.

candied violets

ingredients

1 tablespoon water

1 tablespoon egg
substitute

A handful of violets
(pesticide free)

1 cup superfine sugar

directions

1. In a small custard dish, thin the egg substitute with 1 tablespoon
   of water. (We used egg substitute in place of the traditional
   egg whites because it is thinner and easier for children to apply.)

2. Wash the violets in cold water and gently pat them
   dry with a paper towel. Place the flowers on a
   sheet of waxed paper.

3. Brush a thin layer of the egg mixture onto the
   petals with a small, clean paintbrush.

*A sweet,
simple
delicacy.*

4. Sprinkle the sugar over the violets to cover them
   completely. Shake off the excess sugar. Allow to dry
   completely. Store in an airtight container.

These edible flowers add a delicate finishing touch to your
Valentine cookie box.

old-fashioned sugar pastilles

ingredients

1/4 cup unsalted butter

1/2 cup light corn syrup

3/4 cup granulated
   sugar

1 drop food coloring

2 tablespoons powered
   sugar

1 glass ice cold water

Cooking spray

directions

1. Lightly coat a cookie sheet with cooking spray. Set aside.

2. In a saucepan, combine the butter, corn syrup, and sugar.
   Bring to a boil over medium heat, stirring constantly.
   (Although this is a very simple recipe, adult supervision is
   required. Melted sugar is extremely hot and can cause a seri-
   ous burn.) Continue to boil until a drop of the mixture forms
   a thread when drizzled into a glass of cold water (about 5
   minutes.)

3. Remove from the heat and stir in the food coloring. Pour the
   mixture onto a greased cookie sheet and leave it to cool completely. Once the candy has hardened, break it into pieces
   with a small hammer. Sift powdered sugar over the pastilles
   and surprise your valentine with these old-fashioned sweets.

A shy gesture of friendship.

Be my Valentine?

reflect

Slip a handmade valentine or a simple note into your child's lunch box.

Make a batch of your favorite cookies.

What mementos have you saved that hold special meaning?

Jot down a line from your favorite poem.

together

One of my favorite things about you is....

Alice and Audrey share the prizes from their Easter egg hunt. They proudly display their back yard bouquet of mint, wild onion, quince, pansies and stock in Grandma's china pitcher.

Easter

By early March, I anxiously await the first signs of spring. I know it
has arrived when I see the tiny green shoots of snowdrops and crocus
that push through the ground. Buds swell on flowering trees that welcome
the season with a burst of color. I awake each morning to the song of the
robins that have returned to my front yard.

To celebrate Easter, my children and I find a sun-dappled afternoon,
and take a walk in the woods. They collect armfuls of treasures. Together
we discover the small secrets that Nature quietly reveals with the magic
of a new season.

At home, we weave fresh flowers into Easter baskets. We spend the
next day making natural egg dyes. The small plants we have gathered
in the woods are magically transformed into rich sources of color. All
around us is a storehouse of beautiful things that Nature has provided.

The eggs nestled here could almost be mistaken for the real thing.
Come, take a closer look. These subtle colors were achieved by using natural dyes.

The area covered by the leaf is protected from the dye. When the egg is unwrapped, a white imprint remains.

the dye process

The colors of nature are unique. Part of the fun of decorating eggs with natural dyes is gathering the materials from your own backyard. Flowers, leaves, berries, nut hulls, and even weeds yield surprising colors.

As with all of these projects, take your time and enjoy each other. One child may only be interested in dyeing the eggs, while another will enjoy being a kitchen scientist. The dyes can be made several days in advance and stored in the refrigerator. Gauge the length of the project by the attention span of your child.

before you start

Gather together eggs, an embroidery needle, an enamel pot, vinegar, cheesecloth, a rubber band, and nature's magic ingredients.

directions

1. To prepare the dye bath, fill a glass or enamel pot with two or three cups of plant material. Barely cover it with water (more plant material produces stronger colors.) Simmer for at least 30 minutes. Add water and stir as needed. Transfer to an airtight container and store refrigerated. Strain and heat the liquid dye before using it.

2. Use hard-boiled or blown out eggs. To blow out an egg, make a small hole at each end with an embroidery needle. Use the needle to scramble the yolk inside. Blow the egg until the shell is empty. Carefully wash it with soap and water. Allow the egg to dry. Wipe the eggs with vinegar.

3. One at a time, moisten small leaves and grasses. Press them firmly against the egg. Hold them in place by wrapping the eggs in a 6-inch square of cheesecloth or nylon pantyhose. (Cheesecloth will create a slight textural pattern.) Pull the cloth tight against the egg and secure it with a rubber band or string. Immerse the egg in a container of warm dye. Hold the blown out eggs at the bottom of the pot until they fill with liquid. Some dyes are stronger than others. The process may take only a few moments or several hours. Dyes derived from yellow onionskin, grape hyacinth, and blueberries all provide quick results. Experiment with a wide range of materials. The colors achieved are well worth the wait.

4. It is possible to achieve almost any color using natural dyes. We used (from left to right) blueberries, grape hyacinths, dried marigold blossoms, yellow onion skins (light), yellow onion skins (dark), raspberries, and blackberries.

5. Unwrap the eggs, drain, and let them dry upright. We sign and date ours, to save for years to come.

What a magical and unpredictable process. Each lustrous egg is a unique surprise. Some of our favorites were the results of happy accidents. Enjoy discovering!

Everyday plants yield an infinite choice of colors. The most common materials are magically transformed in the dye pot.
Beets, yellow onions, red onions, blackberries, carrot tops, and parsley are all used as dye stuffs.
You don't need to search for exotic supplies. Experiment with what's in your own backyard.

Easter
dye chart

Parsley
Light green, yellow

Flowering plum red leaves
Fern green

Lupine flowers
Lime green

Lily of the valley
Spring green

Spinach
Olive green, yellow

Red onion skins
Red brown, olive green

Grape hyacinth
Green blue

Blueberries
Indigo blue

Blackberries
Red violet

Raspberries
Pink

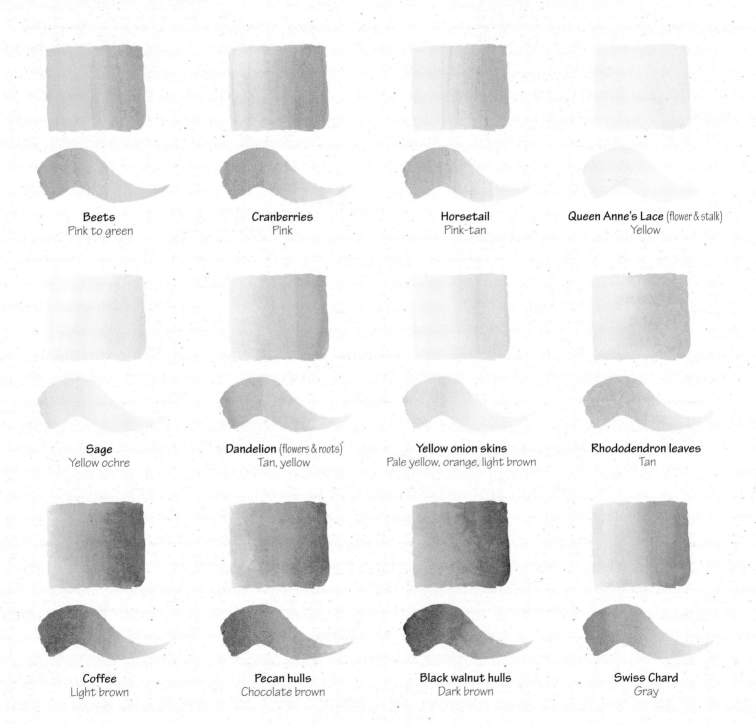

Beets
Pink to green

Cranberries
Pink

Horsetail
Pink-tan

Queen Anne's Lace (flower & stalk)
Yellow

Sage
Yellow ochre

Dandelion (flowers & roots)
Tan, yellow

Yellow onion skins
Pale yellow, orange, light brown

Rhododendron leaves
Tan

Coffee
Light brown

Pecan hulls
Chocolate brown

Black walnut hulls
Dark brown

Swiss Chard
Gray

golden sunrise cake

At Easter time, my family always finds itself with an abundance of blown-out eggs. This modified pound cake recipe is our solution. We serve it on Easter morning with rose petal jelly.

ingredients

4 cups sifted cake flour

1 teaspoon salt

4 teaspoons baking powder

1½ cups butter (3 sticks), softened

3 cups sugar

8 eggs

1 cup milk

2 teaspoons vanilla

1 tablespoon grated orange rind

10-inch, loose bottom, tube pan

directions

1. Preheat oven to 325°.

2. Sift the flour, salt, and baking powder together. Set aside.

3. In a large mixing bowl, cream the butter and the sugar until it is pale and fluffy.

4. Beat in the eggs, one at a time.

5. Add the vanilla and orange zest. Blend thoroughly. Fold in a portion of the flour mixture and alternate with a portion of the milk. Continue until completely blended. Do not over mix.

6. Pour into a generously greased and floured tube pan. Bake at 325° for 1 hour, or until a toothpick inserted comes out clean.

7. Cool completely in the pan. Invert onto a plate and decorate with fresh flowers.

rose water

For centuries, people have used rose water as a perfume, to scent their baths, and to give desserts a sweet hint of flowers. The process of making rose water is similar to making natural dyes. Heat 1 cup of water and 1 cup of freshly picked rose petals (pesticide-free) to a boil. Reduce heat. Cover and simmer for 30 minutes. Strain. Store in a tightly covered decorative glass bottle.

rose petal jelly

ingredients

2 cups tightly packed rose petals (pesticide-free)

1$\frac{1}{2}$ cups water

1 tablespoon lemon juice

$\frac{1}{2}$ package fruit pectin (7 teaspoons)

2 cups sugar

2 (8-ounce) jelly jars

directions

1. Gather the most fragrant, freshly opened roses you can find. Wild roses are best. Deep red roses produce a lovely, brilliant pink color when cooked. The white bases of the petals are bitter. Pinch them off and wash the petals before use.

2. Bring the petals and the water to a boil. Simmer for 20 minutes, stirring occasionally. Strain the liquid into a heatproof glass measuring cup, and reserve the petals.

3. Measure the liquid and add enough water to make 1$\frac{1}{2}$ cups. Stir in the lemon juice and fruit pectin.

4. Return the mixture to the pot and bring it to a boil over high heat. Add the sugar. Bring it to a rolling boil and cook for exactly 1 minute.

5. Immediately remove from the heat and pour into jars. Add a few of the reserved rose petals and stir to prevent them from floating to the top. Seal the jars. Cool. The jelly will keep in the refrigerator for up to two weeks.

Enjoy this flavorful, jewel-tone jelly long after your rose garden has faded.

garden in a basket

Enjoy a little bit of spring while it is still winter outside. A garden in a basket is a fun way to bring the discovery of nature indoors, and is a particularly special gift for someone who is homebound and can't experience the excitement of spring first-hand. For our basket, we chose dianthus, pansy, curly parsley, maiden hair fern, and alyssum. An herb basket is a nice variation for the kitchen windowsill.

before you start

Gather together a basket, a plastic plant dish, potting soil, sheet moss, gravel, 3-inch containers of plants, and a little bit of sunshine.

directions

1. To begin, line a basket with a plastic plant dish, cake pan, or aluminum foil. Make sure the sides are lined as well.

2. Add a thin layer of gravel for drainage.

3. Choose plants in two or three-inch containers. Look for plants with a variety in height, color, and texture. It is fun to sprinkle in a few seeds as well. Remember to start small and leave room for the plants to grow.

4. Leave the plants in their plastic nursery containers. Arrange them in the basket. Cover the surface with potting soil, and then a layer of sheet moss. Let some of the plantings spill over the edge of the basket. Keep it moist with a spritzer bottle and watch your garden grow.

5. Let your children add their own special touches. On walks, collect rocks, pinecones, fossils, shells, honeycombs, or anything that appeals to your child's eye.

These rich earthen tones were produced from dye stuffs
made from Swiss chard (gray), black walnut hulls (dark brown),
dandelion leaves (tan), and blueberries (two shades of blue).

reflect

Wake your family early to watch
the sunrise.

Do you have a favorite
outdoor space?

Spring is about rejuvenation.
If there were one passion in your
life you would like to renew, what
would it be? Would you dust off
your old pastels, strike a few notes
on the neglected piano, or simply
revive a favorite memory like
jumping in puddles with your
child after a spring shower?

together

Something new I'd like to learn....

Children and flowers bring joy to life.

Mother's day

My parents gave us a rose bush when my daughter, Jenny, was born. She napped under a canopy of shade as my husband and I planted the small bush by the fence in our back yard.

A few months later, we took our daughter to meet her great-grandmother, Ollie, for the first time. As a boy, my husband spent many hours helping his grandmother tend to her flowers. On this visit, I watched from the porch as Ollie enlisted my husband to escort her through her garden. With spade in hand, she stopped a moment and pointed. He kneeled and carefully divided a clump of brilliant orange daylilies. That afternoon, she sent us home with many cuttings of her favorite specimens. Next to our rose bush in the backyard, we planted old-fashioned iris, peonies, daylilies, violets, and coral-bells.

My daughter took her first steps as a fountain of pink damask blooms made their debut. When she turned two, we gave her a little plot of her own. Together, we cultivated the soil and sowed seeds of carrots, tomatoes, and sweet peas. As she patted the ground with her tiny hands, she discovered her first earthworm. With eyes like saucers, she watched it wiggle and disappear into the soil.

Together

Throughout the summer, we watched our garden grow. By August, pale blue petunias spilled over a sun-drenched path and the intense fragrance of roses wafted through the warm air. Jenny danced with butterflies as she innocently picked flowers for a small bouquet.

Over the years, our garden has prospered. Each May, I daydream about the unfolding procession of flowers that is yet to come.

Take time to smell the flowers.

Flowers for Grandma.

garden bouquets

Children need only to journey through their own backyard to search for the perfect Mother's Day gift. May gardens explode with colorful choices from which they can make simple, hand-tied bouquets.

before you start

Gather together a wide-necked bottle or vase, a twist tie, cut flowers, a collection of ribbon and handkerchiefs, and your child's magical touch.

directions

1. Begin by picking flowers, grasses, and leaves from the garden. Children will intuitively choose a variety of colors and textures that catch their eye. Try to limit your bouquet to three or four plant materials. As always, simple is best.

2. As a temporary stand, place the flowers in a wide-necked bottle or vase. To keep the arrangement in place, secure a twist tie around the stems and remove the bouquet from the bottle.

3. Vintage handkerchiefs, linen napkins, bandannas or silk ribbons enhance the beauty of fresh picked flowers. Place the bouquet in the center of a handkerchief. Pick both up together. The handkerchief will naturally drape around the stems.

4. Place a 12 to 18-inch ribbon on the table. Place the bouquet in the center of the ribbon and tie a bow to secure the handkerchief and stems.

5. The classic beauty of a bouquet tied with a single ribbon makes for an elegant gift, as well. For a variation, tie the bouquet with variegated grass. What mother can resist being presented with hand-tied flowers and a kiss? In this project, children succeed by making a gift all by themselves.

The gift of a hand-tied bouquet becomes even more special showcased in Mom's favorite Depression glass vase. Roses, begonias, salvia, and cupflowers are simply tied with a silk ribbon.

Sarah and her mother share a quiet moment together.

bunny salad

ingredients

1 head Boston bib lettuce, washed and dried

$^1/_2$ cup cucumber, peeled and sliced

1 cup strawberries, sliced, hulls removed

3 teaspoons poppy seeds

A handful of freshly picked and washed violets or nasturtiums (pesticide free)

directions

1. Combine all ingredients in a large salad bowl.

2. Splash with morning dew lemonade.

Children are always eager to try the fruits (and vegetables) of their labor.

morning dew lemonade

ingredients

1 cup of water

$1^1/_2$ tablespoons of honey

The juice of 1 lemon

directions

1. Combine water and honey and bring to a boil.

2. Add the lemon juice and cool.

crunchy munchy veggie dip

ingredients

1 cup sour cream

1 teaspoon lemon juice

1 carrot, peeled and grated

2 tablespoons chives, chopped

1 sprig of thyme, stems removed

directions

Mix all ingredients. The flavors will intensify when refrigerated overnight.

Serve with fresh garden vegetables and pita bread triangles.

Nothing tastes better than fresh picked vegetables from the garden.

Reminiscent of a bygone era, this herbal nosegay compels the senses with the aroma of basil, lavender, yarrow, and lamb's ear. A white linen napkin encircles the herbs. It is tied together with variegated grass.

"There's rosemary, that's for remembrance. Pray you, love, remember. And there is pansies, that's for thoughts." — Ophelia in Shakespeare's Hamlet

Anyone who has opened a book to find a flower pressed between its pages or has received a dozen red roses from a secret admirer understands the allure of flowers and their scent.

The red rose is a universal symbol of true love. Throughout time, we have ascribed meanings to flowers. The Victorians raised the language of flowers to an art form when they popularized the tussie-mussie, a bouquet of flowers and herbs rich with symbolic meanings.

Even before the Victorian era, we used the language of flowers to convey messages. In Shakespeare's Hamlet, Ophelia's garland of crowflowers, nettles, daisies, and long purples symbolized the young girl's untimely death. Medieval artists often painted the Madonna with white lilies as a metaphor for her purity. As far back as the Roman Empire, Julius Caesar wore a crown of laurels to signify victory.

Flowers and herbs are rich in legends and romance. Their fascination continues even today.

Queen Anne's Lace
Haven

Violet
Faith

Lavender
Devotion

the *Language*

Basil
Good Wishes

Plum Blossom
Happiness

56

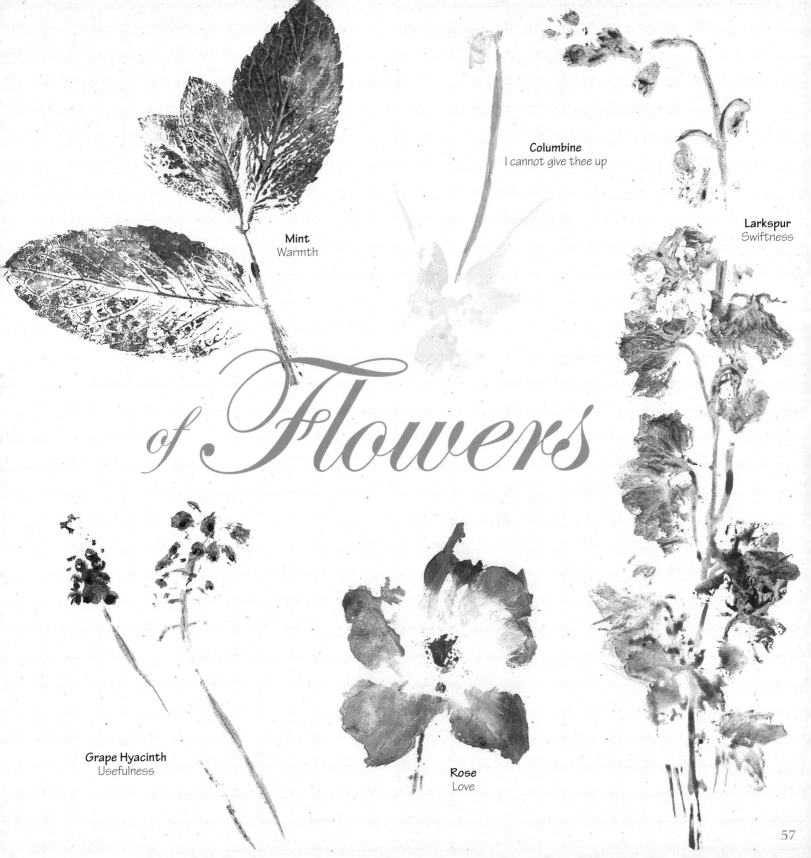

Mint
Warmth

Columbine
I cannot give thee up

Larkspur
Swiftness

of Flowers

Grape Hyacinth
Usefulness

Rose
Love

57

garden activities

Capture a delicate watercolor image of your spring garden. Snip pansies, violets, ferns or any small flower. Mix watercolor paints to match the colors of your flowers and leaves. Gently brush the paint onto the petals. Place the flowers, paint side down, onto watercolor paper. Cover it with a white paper towel. Using the palm of your hand, firmly press to transfer the image onto the paper. (See our prints on page 56.)

Many garden flowers are edible. Try mixing rose petals, violets, nasturtium, snapdragons, or marigolds into a spring salad. Be sure to use flowers that are free of pesticides. Check a field guide for other edible plants from your garden.

Freeze edible flowers or mint in ice cube trays full of water. Add these colorful gems to your next pitcher of lemonade.

You can help the birds build their nests. Hang colorful bits of string or yarn from a tree branch. The birds will use your snippets to weave fanciful color into their nests.

The girls delight in catching butterflies on a sunny afternoon.

Host a ladybug ball. In the spring, many nurseries sell ladybugs. Thoroughly water your plants at dusk and invite the neighborhood to release the ladybugs in your garden. These friends help to control unwanted pests.

Bring a bit of nature indoors. You can force hyacinth, paperwhites, crocus, and tulip bulbs to bloom by placing them in a shallow bowl filled with gravel. Bury the bottom half of the bulb in the gravel. Add just enough water to cover the stones. Place the bowl in a cool dark place for three weeks. When green shoots emerge, move the bowl to a sunny window. Soon fragrant blooms will appear.

To make an herbal bath sachet, place equal amounts of oatmeal, powdered milk and dried herbs (about 2 tablespoons each) in the center of a pretty cloth handkerchief. Tie the bundle with a piece of ribbon. Hang the sachet over the bathtub faucet and let warm water run through it. Enjoy a relaxing, aromatic moment to yourself.

Next time you pull out the paint box, look in your garden to find paintbrushes from nature. Experiment with different brush textures using feathers, ferns, twigs, pine branches, and flowers.

Sprout a family of flower faces. Crack a brown egg in two equal pieces. Use watercolors to paint faces on the eggshells. Fill the eggshells with potting soil. Pat a few seeds into the soil and moisten daily. In a few days your faces will have sprouted fanciful hairstyles. Radish, alfalfa, and zinnia seeds all germinate quickly. In a few weeks, the starts will be ready to plant in your garden.

Preserve cuttings from your May garden by dipping fresh blossoms in paraffin. Place the wax in a tin can. Using a double boiler, heat the wax until it is just melted but cool enough to touch. (Never put paraffin in a pan over direct heat. It will quickly catch fire.) Dip the stems of the flowers into the hot wax. When it has hardened, gently emerse the head of the flower into the melted paraffin. The whole flower should now be sealed in a coating of wax. Let the excess paraffin drip off. Hang the flowers upside down until they are completely dry. Your spring bouquet will keep its color and a hint of perfume for several weeks.

A backyard sleuth.

Attract butterflies and bees to your garden with the sweet nectar of alyssum, clover, daisies, honeysuckle, lavender, lilac, petunias, hibiscus, phlox, and verbena. Watch for new visitors as your flowers begin to bloom.

Watch Nature's transformation from winter to spring by forcing flowering branches in a vase of warm water. Place the freshly cut branches in a sunny indoor spot where you can watch the tiny blossoms appear.

Place a white tulip in a glass vase. Add water and red food coloring. Where does the water go? After a few hours, observe the transformation.

When you find an interesting tree, make a rubbing. Place a piece of paper on top of the bark, run a stick of charcoal over it, and watch the texture appear.

Capture nature's shadows. Place a large piece of paper on the ground where you find interesting shadows. Trace the outline of the shadows.

Mother's helper gives the flowers a drink.

reflect

What did your Grandmother give you that you still cherish?

Has your child ever brought you a hand picked flower?

Press a flower from your garden.

Write your mother a letter. Tell her something you've never told her before.

Make a list of the ways that being a mother has enriched your life. Share it with your children.

together

Mom, some of the ways that you've helped me grow....

A stolen moment.

Father's day

On top of a tall dresser, my father keeps a mahogany box. Its contents are sacred. When I was eight, I crept into his room and, on tiptoes, gazed upward at the box. Determined, I dragged a chair over to the bureau. I climbed onto the chair and stood eye to eye with this mysterious box.

Dad, bottom right.

My hand reached past his pipe stand and brought the box closer into view. Cautiously, I opened the lid and peered inside. Its contents amazed me. Meticulously folded inside a square of notebook paper, I was surprised to find the lucky penny I'd given him. Next to it lay a piece of Doublemint. I was tempted to unwrap the shiny, silver paper, but knew better than to tamper with his things. Underneath his class ring was an old photograph. When I looked closer, I could see it was a picture of his college golf team. I scanned the line of clean cut, young men and found one that looked a lot like me. I set it back in its place and carefully closed the mahogany lid. Climbing down from my perch, I slid the chair into its corner and tiptoed out of the room.

   Looking back on that afternoon, I realized how sentimental my larger than life father could be. I gained many insights that day.

handmade paper

Papermaking is not new. The ancient Egyptians first used paper, made from a plant called papyrus, over 5000 years ago. The variety of papermaking materials is as varied as the whole plant world. Many materials found in the backyard have potential. Use whatever materials are at hand. Grab a brown paper sack and walk outside. You'll find everything you need. Daffodil and lily leaves, hollyhock stalks, cornstalks, and asparagus are among the many plants with which we have experimented. You can even make paper from the weeds that grow between the stones of your garden path.

Use what's available. Shown here are sheets of paper made from asparagus and daffodils.

before you start

Gather together plant materials, a large steel pot, a rolling pin, a terry cloth towel, parchment paper (available at grocery or specialty cooking stores), two 12-inch unglazed terra cotta tiles (available at building supply stores), and a couple of sunny days.

directions

1. In a large porcelain or stainless steel cooking pot, emerse the plant material in water. Simmer for 2-3 hours. We used approximately 50 daffodil leaves for one sheet of paper. (This sounds like a lot, but the leaves actually came from about 10 plants.)

2. Strain. Rinse. Remove the leaves and roll them out with a rolling pin. This helps to break down the fibers.

3. To continue breaking down the fibers, return the pulp to a pot of fresh water and soak it for 3 days. It is best to work outside. When the pulp resembles the consistency of over-cooked asparagus, you are ready to begin making paper.

4. Cover your work surface with a large terry cloth towel. Lay a 12-inch square of parchment paper on top of it.

5. To make a sheet of paper, remove the leaves from the pot one at a time. Hold the leaf between two fingers and gently squeeze out the excess water. Children love to handle the cool, wet, slippery pulp.

6. On top of the parchment paper, lay the leaves in horizontal strips, slightly overlapping each one. Since the leaves naturally taper at one end, alternate the direction of the narrow end. This will help to give you a uniform rectangular shape. The rows will not be perfect. Often the leaves will be slimy, fibrous, and falling apart. This makes

Kit and Cole check on their concoction.

Remember the joy of making mud pies? Making paper has the same irresistible appeal.

the texture and shape of each sheet unique. Each has its own wild and organic look.

7. When you have reached a width of approximately 10-inches, start laying the strips in a perpendicular direction, forming another layer on top of the first.

8. Cover with a second piece of parchment paper. The leaves should now be sandwiched between the two pieces of parchment paper.

9. Use a rolling pin on top of the parchment paper to firmly squeeze out all the excess water. The towel underneath will become soaked. Be sure to roll in the same direction as the top strips, working from the center out.

10. Keep the leaves sandwiched between the two pieces of parchment paper and transfer them to a 12-inch square, unglazed terra cotta tile. Cover with an additional tile. This will help to absorb moisture and keep the freshly made paper flat while it is drying. Several sheets of handmade paper may be stacked on top of each other in this manner. Dry in the warm sun for 48 hours.

11. When the paper is dry, gently peel the fibers away from the parchment. The paper may still retain some moisture. If the paper has not dried completely it will begin to curl.

Honor someone dear to you with a personalized gift. Use your newly made paper to create a scrapbook, or send a special message in a handmade box or card.

Cool and slimy!

We learn as much from our accomplishments as our failures. We made a sheet from iris leaves. Their water-repellent surface was difficult to break down. After soaking the leaves, we pressed them flat. They did not bind to each other. When the leaves were dry, we wove them into a sheet of paper, securing the ends with a dot of white glue. Each plant material is unique, as is each sheet of paper.

collection of treasures

Similar in spirit to the box so many fathers keep on their dresser, I helped my children compile a collection of items to honor their dad on Father's Day. Jenny remembered combing the beach with her dad during her favorite summer vacation. She dug through her stash of seashells and found a perfect sand dollar that they had found that day. Alice chose the ticket stubs from their first baseball game together. They proudly presented him with the compilation of their fondest memories. He valued this gift more than anyone would know. The treasures reminded us all of the importance of sharing time together.

before you start

Gather together two 12-inch square unglazed terra cotta tiles (We found ours at a building supply store for $2.00 each), 2 pieces of 5 x 7-inch mat board, $8\frac{1}{2}$ x 11-inch acid-free card stock, two leather shoelaces (You can find all of these at any large craft store), parchment paper (available at cooking supply or grocery stores), scissors, a hole punch, a drill, and a pile of memories.

directions

To house our collection of treasures, we made a scrapbook out of handmade paper.

1. Cut the mat board into two 5 x 7-inch pieces.

2. Follow the directions for Handmade Paper through step 9. At this stage, you should have a wet sheet of paper, approximately 10-inches square, sandwiched between two pieces of parchment paper. Remove the top layer of parchment and place one piece of the mat board in the center of your handmade paper.

3. Use the bottom piece of parchment to help you wrap the edges of the wet paper around the mat board. The rough ends will almost meet in the middle. Repeat this process so you have two pieces of 5 x 7-inch mat board covered with handmade

Capturing memories.

paper. These will serve as the front and back cover of your scrapbook.

4. Place the covers, side by side, between two fresh sheets of parchment. Sandwich the parchment and covers between two terra cotta tiles. The weight of the tile keeps the covers from warping. Be sure to use unglazed tiles, as they help to absorb moisture. The parchment prevents the paper from sticking to the tile.

5. Take the tiles outside. Dry the paper completely in the warm sun for approximately three days. The covers will warp if removed too soon.

6. Cut the card stock into ten 5 x 7-inch sheets. Stack the sheets and place them horizontally in front of you. Punch two holes, a half-inch from the left-hand side. The holes should be spaced 2-inches apart. Drill corresponding holes in the two covers.

7. Place the paper between the front and back covers so the holes align. Thread the shoelaces through the holes. Leave enough slack in the laces for the pages to open and lie flat on the table. Tie each in a knot.

Making this scrapbook is as easy as wrapping a small package. However this is an extended project. Be patient with nature. Drying times will vary depending on humidity.

It wouldn't be Father's Day without breakfast in bed.

homemade granola

ingredients

3 cups old-fashioned
   rolled oats

1 cup walnuts or
   pecans, chopped

1 cup wheat germ

$1/2$ cup brown sugar

$1/4$ cup whole-wheat
   flour

$1/4$ cup vegetable oil

$1/4$ cup honey

$1/4$ cup molasses

$1/4$ cup water

1 tablespoon vanilla
   extract

1 cup raisins

directions

1. Preheat oven to 325°.

2. Combine all of the ingredients except the raisins.

3. Spread on a lightly greased cookie sheet.

4. Bake 30 minutes. Check and stir occasionally.

5. Remove from the oven and add the raisins. Let mixture
   cool completely. The granola will crisp as it cools. Store
   in an airtight container.

Snack on it by the handful
or serve with fresh berries,
yogurt, or milk.

This is a very easy recipe.
You can adjust the
ingredients to your
own taste. Kids love it
because it tastes like
oatmeal cookies.

Rough housing with Dad.

Another Father's Day tradition.

reflect

What small tokens hold special
meaning for you?

Do you have a secret hiding place
for special treasures? Did you
as a child?

Were there rituals you did only
with your Father? Did he read to
you? Did he take you to baseball
games? Did you walk the
dog together?

What did you learn from your Dad?

together

Dad, you were there for me when....

We celebrated Independence Day with American classics:
watermelon, lemonade, blueberry muffins, and home baked cookies.

the Fourth of July

Last Fourth of July, we rounded up our neighborhood friends and gathered for an old-fashioned picnic in the park. The sprawling arms of an old oak tree made a canopy of shade over baskets brimming with summer treats. Lucy couldn't resist poking her finger into the blueberry pie. This seemed the perfect moment to begin our pie-eating contest. We awarded blue ribbons for "messiest," "best manners," "biggest mouthful," and "first to the bottom." Everyone was a winner!

John grabbed a baton and led a procession of toddlers in an imaginary marching band. A group of older kids ventured down to the creek and crafted sailboats out of driftwood and twigs.

As we relaxed on the lawn, the afternoon's heat soon gave way to a cool evening breeze. One by one, the fireflies appeared. As we heard the muffled sound of fireworks in the distance, the fireflies began a display of their own. Their dancing patterns of light created magic against the summer sky.

A free spirit.

comets, rockets, and whirls

These old-fashioned American fireworks are simple enough for anyone to enjoy. Even the youngest children are engaged as active participants in the festivities.

rockets

Save a few corncobs from your last summer picnic. Leave the tapered ends in tact and be sure to remove the stalks. Allow them to dry in the sun for about a week. Using a $1/4$-inch drill bit, have an adult drill a hole in the blunt end of the corncob. Work the quills of three turkey feathers into the hole. There are two ways to throw a rocket. First, hold it by the feathers and flip it high into the air. It will helicopter back to earth. Second, throw the rocket through the air as you would a dart. See who can throw theirs the farthest. Some will fly long and straight. Others will twist and dive.

comets

Cut three strips of crepe paper, each 2-yards long. Lay two strips out on a table to form an X. Lay the third piece horizontally across the center of the X to form an asterisk. Place a rubber ball in the center of the crepe paper. Gather the crepe paper around the ball and secure it with a rubber band. Throw comets into the sky or across the lawn to a partner. Their paper tails spiral through the air and make unpredictable twists and turns as they bounce to the ground.

streamers

Cut a 2-yard length of red, white, or blue ribbon. Find the center and tie it around the end of a 2-foot long stick or wooden dowel. The graceful streamers of these simple toys will mesmerize toddlers.

whirls

Using an 8-inch square of colored paper cut the corners off to make a circle. Starting in the center, draw a spiral to the outside edge. Cut along the line of the spiral. Weight the center of the spiral with a paper clip. Perch yourself in the branch of a favorite climbing tree or on your father's shoulders. Drop the whirls from above and watch them corkscrew to the ground.

The boys launched their sailboats to prove they were sea worthy.

miniature sailboats

In the heat of the afternoon, find relief by wandering down to the creek for an impromptu regatta. Search your surroundings for anything that looks remotely seaworthy. Find a bit of water, kick off your shoes, and set sail. Anything can qualify for a boat: a curled leaf, a buoyant stick, or even a blade of grass.

For a larger boat, start with a flat piece of bark. Mulch bark works well because it is lightweight. After determining that your bark will float, make a hole directly in the center of the boat. For a mast, fit a thin, straight twig into the hole. The twig should be about the same length as the bark. A mast that is too tall will capsize the boat. If you need to make your mast more stable, place a dab of mud in the hole before attaching the twig. Fashion a sail out of an interesting leaf or dried cornhusk.

Experiment with different sails. Some will tip the boat over, while others will catch the wind with ease.

For a miniature sailing vessel, start with half of a walnut shell or a milkweed pod. Fill the hull with a bit of mud or clay and attach a sail made from a feather or a flower petal. Wait for an afternoon breeze. Set your boats afloat and watch them drift.

Good times and old-fashioned American spirit turned an afternoon into a lively celebration.

mom's blueberry muffins

ingredients

2 cups sifted flour

1 tablespoon baking powder

$1/4$ teaspoon salt

$1/2$ cup sugar

1 egg

1 cup milk

$1/2$ cup melted butter

1 cup fresh blueberries

directions

1. Preheat oven to 425°.

2. Sift and measure the flour.

3. In a large mixing bowl, combine the flour, baking powder, salt, and sugar.

4. In the microwave, melt the butter in a heatproof glass measuring cup.

5. Add the egg and milk to the dry ingredients. Stir just enough to combine. Add the melted butter. Mix. The batter should remain lumpy. Add the blueberries and stir gently.

6. Spoon the batter into a greased and floured muffin tin, filling each about $2/3$ full. Bake for approximately 25 minutes or until the tops are golden brown. Yields 18 muffins.

great grandmother borland's sand tarts

ingredients

2 cups (4 sticks) softened butter

2 cups sugar

2 eggs well beaten

3 cups twice sifted flour

1 teaspoon vanilla

$1/4$ cup sugar mixed with 1 teaspoon cinnamon

$1/2$ cup finely chopped pecans

1 additional egg, white only (do not beat)

directions

1. Preheat the oven to 350°.

2. Cream the butter and sugar until light and fluffy.

3. Add the eggs. Stir. Add the vanilla.

4. Add the sifted flour, a little at a time.

5. Drop the dough from the tip of a teaspoon, about 2-inches apart, onto an ungreased cookie sheet.

6. Place a small dish with the cinnamon/sugar mixture and another dish with the egg white next to your cookie sheet.

7. Using your finger, dab a little bit of the egg white onto the top of each cookie. Sprinkle with a small amount of the cinnamon/sugar mixture and chopped pecans.

8. Bake 6-8 minutes. Be careful. These cookies burn easily.

Nothing tastes better than Grandma's cookies.

strawberry lemonade

ingredients

Juice of 6 lemons

6 medium strawberries

3/4 cup sugar

4 cups water

directions

1. Wash the strawberries and remove the green tops.

2. Place the strawberries in a blender with the lemon juice, sugar, and 2 cups of water. Blend on low for 30 seconds.

3. Pour the mixture into a pitcher with the remaining water and serve over ice.

Make it. Bake it. Have a pie eating contest.
We pulled out all the stops and gave each child a pie of their own.

We detected a mischievous glint in the childrens' eyes as we dressed them in old white shirts and rolled up their sleeves. A bucket of water and a basket of towels made for an easy clean up.

Being encouraged to do something that is normally off limits brought out the competitive spirit in all the kids.

In our contest, everyone was a winner. Our pie eaters proudly displayed their ribbons for First to the Bottom, Messiest, Best Manners, and Biggest Bite.

reflect

Each family has its own heritage. How did your family come to this country?

What made summer magical to you as a child?

When the neighborhood kids gathered, what did you play?

Read *The Adventures of Tom Sawyer* with your family.

together

Simple pleasures....

This happy fellow kept a faithful watch over our Halloween celebration.

Halloween

Alice adorned her hat with autumn grasses from the harvested fields.

To take advantage of the last days of autumn, we planned an outdoor Halloween party at our family farm. This gave us an opportunity to bring our friends together in an informal setting before the hectic holiday season.

The children grew excited as we drove past the harvested fields of rural farmland, the grazing cattle, and brimming roadside stands. The sights and smells of the country awoke their spirits of adventure and they burst from the car as soon as we stopped at the end of the dirt road.

As they explored their surroundings, the adults began to set up. Our party centered on the activity of making scarecrows. We brought out baskets piled high with faded denim coveralls, straw hats, and flannel shirts. The children enthusiastically costumed themselves as well as the scarecrows. They collected autumn grasses and flowers and wove them

Scott playfully kept the crows away.

into straw hats to take home as mementos.

The country setting and the crisp autumn air inspired many activities. Sack races, a tug of war, and a scavenger hunt kept everyone busy throughout the afternoon.

As the day came to a close, our guests enjoyed an Indian summer sunset. We bundled sleepy children into cars and returned home with warm recollections of an afternoon shared with special friends.

Through the eyes of the children, a bale of hay was a huge mountain ready for climbing.

Scraps of yarn and felt brought this character's personality to life.

the scarecrow

The children quickly transformed themselves into human scarecrows. We provided baskets of raffia Hawaiian skirts, cut into quarters, to tie on their wrists. To take the snap from the air, they dressed in flannel shirts.

Stuffing a scarecrow is simple. We gave each of ours a unique personality by using harvest materials to create their faces.

before you start

Gather together an 8-inch Styrofoam ball, raffia, a glue gun, corn husks, a box of golden yellow dye, straight pins, safety pins, yarn and felt scraps, charcoal, oil pastels, 2 pairs of panty hose, polyester batting or hay, 1 metal fence stake, rope, old clothing, and a pocket full of whimsy.

directions

1. For the head, cover an 8-inch Styrofoam ball with raffia. Starting at the top, use a low melt glue gun to attach a few strands at a time, until the entire sphere is covered. Tie all of the loose ends together at the bottom, to form the neck.

2. Make the hair by soaking dried cornhusks in a bath of golden yellow dye. Follow the directions on the box. The dye intensifies the color of the cornhusks and makes them more pliable. Tie a knot in the middle of each husk and let it dry. Attach them to the head with a glue gun and secure the hat with straight pins.

3. A face made of yarn and felt brings the scarecrow's personality to life.

4. For the second scarecrow, cover a Styrofoam ball with dried cornhusks. Add a face with charcoal and oil pastels. For a finishing touch, use a carrot for his nose and crown him with autumn leaves.

5. Children will delight in stuffing his body with hay. City dwellers might consider using polyester batting or crumpled newspaper instead of hay. This makes for a more flexible body when stuffed into pantyhose. Use one pair of panty hose for the legs and one for the arms. We then safety pinned the two sections together at the waist.

6. To stand him upright, start with two crossed sticks. We used a metal fence stake as our upright, and secured our fellow with a rope.

Admiring the fruits of our labor, we stood back and waited for the crows.

Together

After they scattered and tossed the straw, some of the hay finally made it into the scarecrows.

Our second friend proudly displayed a carrot nose and a crown of crimson leaves.

Parents spread a simple buffet on the tailgate of a vintage pickup truck. Friends naturally gathered around a hearty offering of spiced cider, corn muffins, and meat pies. For a centerpiece, children delighted in collecting corn silk and dried seedpods that they placed in a vintage crock.

hearty meat pies

ingredients

FILLING

1 pound beef stew meat, cut into 1-inch cubes

1 tablespoon dried rosemary, finely chopped

1 teaspoon dried sage

Salt and ground pepper to taste

$1/3$ cup flour

2 tablespoons olive oil

2 cups beef stock

1 large potato, cut into cubes

3 large carrots, peeled and sliced

3 stalks celery, sliced

directions

FILLING

1. In a plastic bag, toss together the beef, rosemary, sage, salt, and pepper.

2. Add the flour to the bag and toss again.

3. Heat the oil in a heavy stockpot, over medium high heat. Shake the excess flour from the stew meat and add the meat to the oil. Brown the meat.

4. Add the beef stock to the pot and bring it to a boil. Stir to deglaze the pot.

5. Add the vegetables. Cover. Reduce heat to low and simmer for 2 hours. Stir occasionally.

hearty meat pies (cont.) page 98

hearty meat pies (cont.)

ingredients

CRUST

4 cups all-purpose flour

1 teaspoon salt

1 cup shortening, chilled

1 cup cold water

directions

CRUST

1. Sift the flour and the salt into a large mixing bowl.

2. Cut the shortening into the flour mixture until it resembles coarse meal.

3. Add the water, a little at a time, and stir with a fork until well blended.

4. Divide the dough into two equal balls. On a floured board, roll each ball out to $1/4$-inch thickness.

ASSEMBLING IT ALL

1. Preheat the oven to 350°.

2. Cut a 6-inch circle out of a piece of paper.

3. Using the paper as a guide, cut six circles out of the dough.

4. Use a cookie cutter to cut out eighteen autumn leaves from the remaining dough.

5. In the center of each circle, place $1/4$ cup of the beef stew. Brush the edges of each circle with a little bit of the beaten egg. Fold the circles in half and crimp the edges with the tines of a fork. Brush the top of the meat pies with more of the beaten egg.

6. Arrange three of the dough leaves on the top of each pie. Brush with egg and transfer the pies onto a lightly greased cookie sheet.

7. Bake at 350° for 30-45 minutes, until golden brown.

Zack took a break to enjoy a hearty snack.

corn bread muffins

ingredients

¹/₄ cup all-purpose flour

³/₄ cup yellow corn meal

¹/₄ cup sugar

2 teaspoons baking powder

A pinch of salt

1 egg

¹/₄ cup cooking oil

³/₄ cup milk

¹/₄ cup dried apricots, finely chopped

The grated zest of one small orange.

directions

1. Preheat the oven to 400°.

2. In a large bowl, mix together the flour, corn meal, sugar, baking powder and salt.

3. In another bowl, mix together the remaining ingredients.

4. Pour the wet mixture into the dry mixture. Stir until moist, but still lumpy.

5. Pour into a greased muffin tin.

6. Bake at 400° for 20 minutes.

Jenny and Travis were neck and neck as they finished the sack race.

The country setting and the crisp autumn air inspired many activities.

As the last rays of sunlight pierced the crisp autumn air,
we said good-bye to special friends.

reflect

Do you remember any games
or activities from Halloween
parties of your childhood?

Did you ever play pretend?

If you could masquerade as
anyone, who would it be?

As a family, write a ghost story.

together

It was a dark and stormy night....

A walk in the woods.

Thanksgiving

Listen to the sounds of the season. Dried leaves rustle under foot, birds call, and squirrels chatter while collecting nuts. The air is crisp as the last lingering days of Indian summer slip away. Amidst animals scurrying to prepare for winter, my girls stuff their pockets full of acorns. They stop to crack a nut and examine what's inside. My eldest runs ahead and plunges herself into a pile of fallen leaves. We all dive in after her. We toss armfuls of leaves into the air and watch the golden shapes catch the wind. Autumn's rich landscape is full of nature's bounty.

   To welcome friends and family, wreaths, rich with fall's ornament, festoon the entryway of my home. Our family celebrates, much as the first settlers did, by giving thanks for nature's harvest.

An autumn wreath offers the prospect of a warm and friendly welcome. We invited a group of four year-olds to help us string dried apples, oranges, and lemons.

golden apple wreath

The wreath is a symbol of the continuous cycle of nature. It signifies fellowship and hospitality throughout the holidays. Fall's abundance of natural materials and the wreath's simple circular shape inspire children to create endless variations.

before you start

Gather together a wire coat hanger, pliers, raffia, 1-pound each of apples, oranges, and lemons, salt, lemon juice, and a kitchen full of warmth and good company.

directions

1. In a shallow glass baking dish, combine 1 cup of lemon juice with 1 tablespoon of salt.

2. You will need 1 pound each of red apples, oranges, and lemons. Thinly slice the fruit into circles, leaving the cores and peels in place.

3. Soak the fruit slices in the lemon juice mixture for 10 minutes. Drain the slices in a colander, reserving the excess liquid for additional batches.

4. Place the slices on cookie sheets.

Dry them in a 200° oven for 6 to 8 hours. Leave the oven door open slightly for the first few hours to let the excess moisture escape. The apples are finished when they are pliable, not crisp.

5. Remove the hook from a wire coat hanger and shape the wire into a circle. String the fruit onto the hanger until all but 2-inches of wire on each end is covered. With pliers, form a hook on each end and link the two hooks together. Evenly space the dried fruit around the wreath and finish with a raffia bow.

6. If you like, add cinnamon sticks and baby's breath with a low melt glue gun. For variation, experiment with dried sweet potatoes, peppers, beets and green apples.

We invited several four-year olds and their mothers to make these wreaths at a holiday party. This is a simple project for young children. The group easily completed these beautiful wreaths in a half-hour. The aroma of drying apples and spicy cinnamon sticks added warmth and cheer to our gathering.

songbird wreath

My kids have always faithfully kept track of the birds that visit our backyard. They learned this from their grandparents, who for many years, have provided the birds with plenty of food throughout the winter. We especially like this wreath because it brings many varieties right to our window.

before you start

Gather together a 12-inch grapevine wreath, raffia, peanut butter, birdseed, pinecones, sunflowers seed heads, dried corn, and a quiet hour for watching.

directions

1. Use a 12-inch grapevine wreath as a base.

2. Tie a large sunflower seed head to the top of the wreath with raffia.

3. Coat several small pinecones with peanut butter and roll them in birdseed. Attach them to the wreath with raffia.

4. Offer your feathered guests an assortment of tasty treats. They will especially like small ears of Indian corn, dried fruit, shafts of wheat, millet, or any seed bearing native grasses. The ingredients will change as the harvest season progresses.

5. Secure everything to the wreath by tying it with raffia or by tucking it into the twisted grapevine.

Cedar waxwings, cardinals, chickadees, sparrows, red wing blackbirds, and finches were attracted to our wreath. Watch for regular visitors at yours.

With cooler days approaching, birds and animals begin to prepare for the winter. The bounty of the season provided us with berries, seeds, fruits, and nuts for our bird-feeding wreath. Hang it in a window to enjoy many months of bird watching.

Celebrate family gatherings with this colorful magnolia wreath.

celebration wreath

Every member of the family contributed to this fanciful wreath of painted leaves. No matter the age or skill level of the painter, each leaf is integral to the beauty of the whole.

before you start

Gather together an 18-inch diameter straw wreath, magnolia leaves, high gloss acrylic paint, $3\frac{1}{2}$-yards of $\frac{1}{4}$-inch elastic, 1 straight pin, and a child's artistic inspiration.

directions

1. Fill a large grocery sack with magnolia leaves.

2. Paint the leaves with high gloss acrylic paint. (We used magenta, orange, yellow, and blue.) Let them dry overnight.

3. As a base, use an 18-inch diameter straw wreath.

4. Wrap the wreath with the elastic. Start by securing one end of the elastic to the top of the wreath with a long straight pin. Wrap the elastic around the wreath at 3-inch intervals. The elastic should be snug against the straw, but not too tight. Once you have gone all the way around the wreath, tie the ends of the elastic together.

5. Starting at the top and working clockwise, tuck the stems of two or three leaves into each band of elastic. Try to arrange the leaves so that no elastic or straw shows. Once you finish, small leaves work best to hide any bare spots. This wreath should take about 15 minutes to assemble. Use any leaves that are leftover to make a cheerful Thanksgiving centerpiece or garland. Improvise.

autumn adventures

Walk down a woodland path into autumn's canopy of spectacular colors. Trees tower overhead. Falling leaves herald the changing season. Look up. A squirrel's nest reveals itself to the world below. Under foot, damp leaves shelter a world of insects hard at work. The forest holds many secret treasures waiting to be discovered.

On your next walk in the woods, take along a magnifying glass, tweezers, collection baskets, and a field guide. Experience the world around you.

Capture autumn's rich hues in a delicate tapestry of leaf imprints. Place a piece of unbleached muslin or linen on top of a few sheets of newsprint. Collect leaves and place them face down on the fabric. Cover with wax paper. Pound them with a hammer or mallet to transfer the patterns and colors to the fabric. Choose the freshest materials available because dry leaves do not have enough pigment to make a clear print. Experiment with different leaves. To set the colors, combine $\frac{1}{2}$ cup of salt with 3 gallons of warm water. Soak the fabric for 15 minutes.

Weave a collage from your autumn gatherings. Find a branch with at least two forks and wrap twine or raffia back and forth between the twigs. Weave feathers, leaves, grasses, moss, and seeds into the branches to showcase your findings from an afternoon of foraging.

Even the youngest of children enjoy collecting mementos on a nature walk. Make a bracelet by wrapping a strip of masking tape loosely around your wrist with the sticky side out. Press pebbles, bark, and lichen onto the tape. Create a mosaic of textures as you walk.

Study the different birds in your area. Look for feathers on your next walk. At home, coat each feather with black ink and sandwich it between two pieces of white paper. Press firmly and evenly with the palm of your hand to record its impression.

Accent your walkway or garden with miniature luminarias suspended from the trees. Hollow out apples, small squashes, or gourds. Carve a pattern with a vegetable peeler, a leather punch, an ice pick, or a nail. Around the top edge, use a nail to punch three equally spaced holes. Thread a 12-inch piece of twine through each hole and tie the three ends together. Place a tea candle inside the lantern and hang it from a branch. To make an impact, use several throughout the yard. The glow from these dancing patterns will warm a harvest night.

Witt and Katie at the orchard.

fruit leather

ingredients

2 tablespoons lemon
  juice

2 tablespoons honey

2 cups applesauce

Cooking spray

directions

1. Preheat oven to warm, 200°.

2. In a medium sized mixing bowl, combine the lemon juice and the honey.

3. Stir in the applesauce.

4. Coat a 13 x 9-inch glass baking dish with cooking spray. Pour in the mixture and spread evenly.

5. Place the baking dish in the warm oven. Cook for 12 hours, or until the fruit leather is pliable but not brittle.

6. Cut the fruit leather into strips and store it in an airtight container.

Celebrate the world around you.

reflect

Take a walk in the woods.

Feed the birds.

What are your family's favorite Thanksgiving recipes?

Who did you most look forward to seeing at Thanksgiving dinner when you were a child?

What family member do you most resemble?

together

Give thanks....

Garlands of glass beads, gilded nuts and gingerbread men are the culmination of a season of activity. They enhance the magical setting for this much awaited night.

Christmas

As a child, my Christmas began the day after Thanksgiving. Our family took a drive in the country. My parents gave the children the honor of finding the perfect Christmas tree.

To this day, I enjoy planning a trip to the family farm with my own children. The tree is never quite perfect, inevitably too bulky or tall. Often, it is crooked and sparse. Nevertheless, I delight in seeing the look on the faces of my children when they find their favorite tree.

The magic comes when we transform this lonely cedar into a showpiece. Each ornament holds memories of a Christmas past, and new keepsakes are precious additions to our treasured collection.

My favorites are the old-fashioned mercury glass ornaments that I grew up with as a child. My children love the ornaments given to them, as a tradition each year, by their special Aunt Betsy. The anticipation of unwrapping the tissue is only surpassed by the joy of rediscovering these old friends. As each treasure emerges, we give it a place of honor on the tree.

Perhaps most precious are the ornaments we've made ourselves. Each year we sign and date one to save for our family tree. As we reveal each keepsake, I reflect on the wonder of watching my children grow.

Any age child will enjoy making gingerbread men. While Jenny helped to string the garland, my three-year-old enjoyed counting and sorting the gingerbread men.

gingerbread man garlands

ingredients

$\frac{1}{4}$ cup shortening

$\frac{1}{2}$ cup dark brown sugar

$\frac{1}{2}$ cup dark molasses

$\frac{1}{4}$ cup water

4 cups all-purpose flour

$\frac{1}{4}$ teaspoon ground cloves

$\frac{1}{2}$ teaspoon cinnamon

1 teaspoon ginger

$\frac{1}{2}$ teaspoon salt

Small gingerbread man cookie cutter

Twelve yards of $1\frac{1}{4}$-inch satin ribbon

A child's embroidery needle

directions

1. Preheat the oven to 350°.

2. In a large mixing bowl, blend the shortening and the sugar.

3. Beat in the molasses and the water.

4. Add the flour, cloves, cinnamon, ginger, and salt. Mix well.

5. Separate the dough into two balls and refrigerate for one hour.

6. On a floured board, roll each ball out to $\frac{1}{4}$-inch thickness. With a small cookie cutter, press out the gingerbread men and place them on a greased cookie sheet. To make quarter-inch holes for stringing the garland, use the eraser end of a new pencil. These holes will later shrink during baking. Press two holes into the chest of each gingerbread man.

7. Bake at 350° for eight to ten minutes.

8. Cut the satin ribbon into twelve pieces, each one-yard in length. Tie a knot two-inches from the end of each piece. Thread the other end through a child's embroidery needle.

9. When the gingerbread men have cooled, let the children group them into piles of ten. Thread them, one at a time, onto the ribbon. The hands of the gingerbread men should almost touch. After stringing the tenth man, tie a knot in the ribbon. Do not be discouraged if a few gingerbread men break. Toss the broken pieces together with a few sprigs of pine for a Christmas potpourri.

The smell of ginger and allspice conjures up memories of helping my grandmother prepare for Christmas. We hung these fragrant garlands as a nostalgic tribute to Christmases past.

christmas pears in spiced cider

ingredients

4 firm but ripe Bartlett pears

$1^1/_4$ cups apple cider

Peel of $^1/_2$ lemon, white pith removed

Juice of 1 lemon

$^1/_4$ cup sugar

1 cinnamon stick

6 cloves

16 allspice berries

directions

1. Peel the pears, leaving the stem in place. From the bottom, carefully remove the core with a paring knife. Cut a thin slice off of the base of each pear so that it will stand upright.

2. Combine the cider, lemon peel, lemon juice, sugar, and spices in a saucepan.

3. Bring the liquid to a boil. Reduce heat. Add the pears, cover, and simmer until tender. Cooking time will vary depending on the ripeness of the pears.

4. Transfer the pears to a serving dish. To reduce the liquid, bring the cider to a boil for 5 minutes.

5. Pour the hot liquid over the pears. Cool. Cover and refrigerate overnight.

6. Garnish with fresh mint leaves and serve.

The sweet smell of clove studded pomanders fills the room with the aroma of Christmas. These were made by pressing whole cloves into a fresh orange.

gilded nut garlands

Stringing garlands is an age-old Christmas tradition. Children of all ages can partici-pate. Sitting around the kitchen table or the warmth of a fireplace sets the mood for relaxed conversation. While busy hands string garlands, take advantage of this special time together.

before you start

Gather together a variety of nuts, a craft brush, a bottle of gold leaf adhesive size, 1 pack of gold leaf sheets (both available at craft supply stores), a drill, a long embroidery needle, heavy-duty thread, and several nimble fingers.

directions

1. Gather a variety of nuts. Pecans, walnuts, hazelnuts, and almonds all work well. Each adds an interesting variety of texture and shape to the garland.

2. Have an adult drill through each nut. Before you start, be sure to put a board underneath. Have plenty of extra nuts on hand. A few will crack and break.

3. Cover the table with newspaper. Working in a well-ventilated area, use a craft brush or small sponge to dab on a thin coat of gold leaf adhesive size to the surface of each nut. Work quickly, as your hands will soon become sticky. You do not need to be exact. As the adhesive begins to dry, it will change from milky white to clear in color. It will take approximately one hour until you can apply the gold leaf.

4. Wash brushes immediately in warm soapy water.

5. Gold leaf comes in packets, usually twenty-five sheets to a package. Originally, eighteen-karat gold leaf was used to gild furniture, picture frames, antiques, and art objects. Today, inexpensive leaf is available at craft stores in gold, silver, and copper colors. Gently, use your fingertips to lift the very thin sheets of foil. The leaf will adhere immediately to the tacky surface of the nut. Don't worry if it wrinkles and crumples. This only adds to the interesting textures of the surface. Instead of gilding the entire

nut, try a more free form approach, which leaves part of the natural surface of the nut visible. This is a very quick and easy process for children because there are no mistakes, only happy accidents that make each nut unique.

6. You may want to save the stringing of the garland for another day. Thread a long embroidery needle with heavy duty, buttonhole thread. Use short lengths of twenty-four inches. These have less of a tendency to tangle. Our finished garland took a seven-year-old one half-hour to complete.

The shape and texture of each nut was enhanced with a glimmer of gold.

glass bead garlands

Make a luminous garland of glass beads. Its multi-faceted jewel tones will sparkle in the light of a frosty window or enhance the reflections of shimmering Christmas tree lights.

before you start

Gather together a variety of glass beads, muffin tins or small bowls, fine gauge beading wire, craft scissors, and sparkling conversation.

directions

1. Glass beads are available at craft or import stores. Choose a variety of colors and sizes.

2. Muffin tins or small bowls serve to contain and sort loose beads.

3. A fine gauge beading wire eliminates the use of a needle. Using craft scissors cut the wire into 18 to 24-inch lengths. This will make the garlands easier for small children to handle and the shorter wire will be less likely to tangle.

4. Tie a knot around the first bead to secure it.

5. String the beads randomly. By choosing their favorites, children naturally vary both the color and the size.

6. Finish the garland by looping the wire back through the last bead and tying a knot.

7. Drape the garlands individually or join several with satin ribbons.

The attention span of my five-year-old was about one half-hour. Older children will become more involved and want to continue longer. Again, this is a project that we worked on for several days.

Every year Alice and her father, as a gift to me, create a centerpiece for our Christmas table. This year, they presented me with a few cuttings of Nandina from our backyard, placed in an antique silver pitcher.

reflect

*Did you ever receive an
 unexpected gift?*

*What family traditions have
endured through the years?*

*What new traditions have you
started with your family?*

*Write down your favorite
Christmas carol.*

together

*If I could give you anything in
the world...*

index

Together

creating family traditions

rondi hillstrom davis

janell sewall oakes

NINE
TWENTY
PRESS